Structured Programming using C

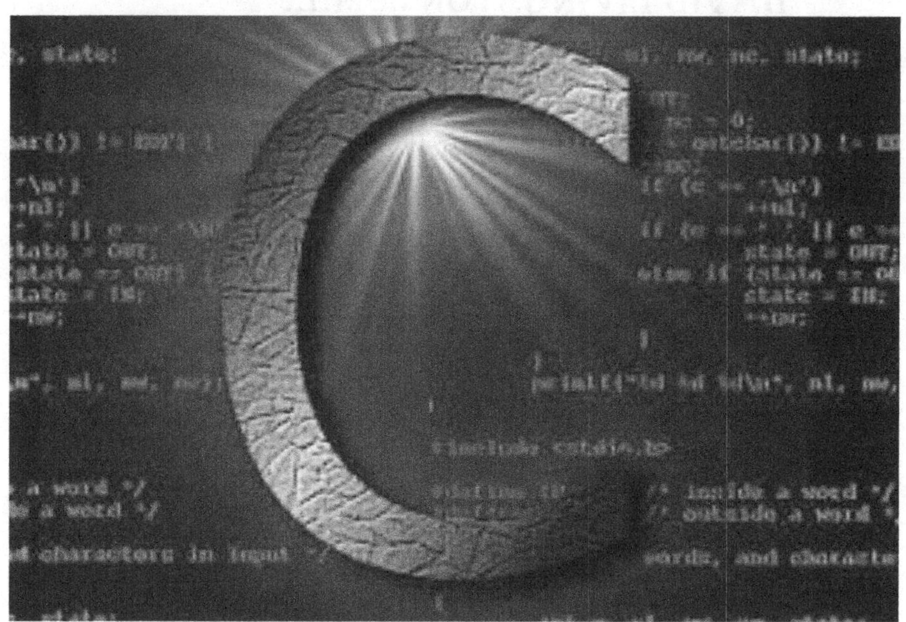

DAVID LIVINGSTON J, M.E.

ISBN # : 978-93-5346-400-4

Written and Published By:

DAVID LIVINGSTON J, M.E.
FFY Educational Services,
Coimbatore—28

Mobile:

99942 86194

Our Websites:

http://ffy.vpweb.in

http://jdlcse.blogspot.com

TABLE OF CONTENT!

SECTION 1

SECTION 2

TABLE OF CONTENT!

SECTION 3

SECTION I

Basics of Computer Programming

This section introduces some of the basic concepts involved in Programming. It includes the following chapters:

Introduction to Programming Languages

Software Development Life Cycle (SDLC)

Structured Programming

Object Oriented Programming

Planning a Program using Flowchart

Planning a Program using Pseudo Code

Introduction to C Language

Fundamental Elements of C

Chapter 1

INTRODUCTION TO PROGRAMMING LANGUAGES

Programming languages are coding schemes using which instructions can be given to a computer system for automating some of the tasks performed manually in our day to day life. Using computer languages such as C/C++, professionals develop software of different kinds which include Operating Systems and Application Software.

Various Programming Languages of Computer

Software developed using a programming language can help solve a particular problem using computer. Programming languages provide a programmer with a set of keywords, symbols and a system of rules for constructing statements that can be executed by a computer.

The symbols and keywords are having special meaning in the language. The set of rules (called syntax) dictate how the symbols should be combined into statements capable of conveying meaningful instructions to the CPU.

Generation of Programming Languages

The **First Generation** programming language is machine language, which makes use of binary symbols (0s and 1s) for coding. As machine language is the language of the CPU, programs written using machine language can be understood and executed directly by the CPU.

Second Generation Language (2GL) overcomes some of the difficulties faced by programmers of machine language by replacing the binary digits with symbols. Thus, the programs written using second generation language are in more readable form than that of the machine language. Second generation language is also called as **Assembly language**, since assembly language programs are converted into binary language coding before their execution with the help of a language translator named **Assembler**.

Third Generation Languages (3GL) are high level languages that use English-like statements and commands. Some of the third generation languages are: BASIC,

COBOL, FORTRAN, C, C++ and Java. 3GL languages are easier to learn and use than machine and assembly languages because they use commands that resemble everyday human communication.

With third-generation programming languages, each statement in the language translates into several instructions in the machine language. A special software program called **Compiler** converts programmer's source code into machine language instructions consisting of binary digits, as shown in below figure:

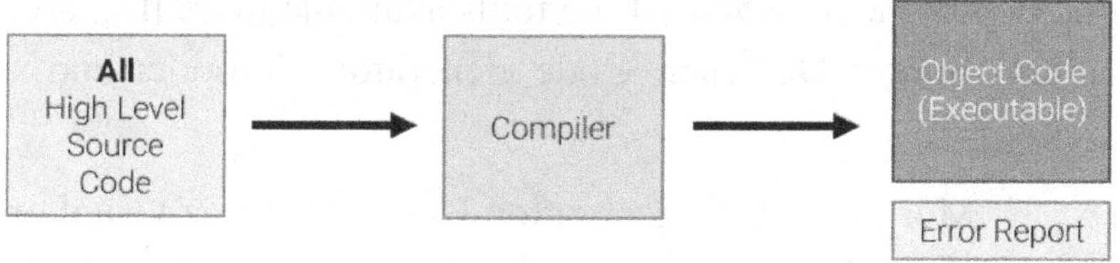

The Role of a Compiler

Fourth Generation Languages (4GL) are languages that support Client/Server technology. 4GL languages have the following characteristics which distinguish them from the third generation languages:

1. Provide features for storing and accessing information from a database.

2. Emphasize what output results are desired rather than how programming statements are to be written.

3. Provide the tools for designing the User Interface screens easily.

4GL languages are of two types: Front-ends and Back-ends. Front-ends are tools that include visual development tools like PowerBuilder, Delphi, Essbase, Focus, Powerhouse and SAS. Back-ends are Database

Management Systems (DBMS) such as MS Access, SQL Server, and Oracle. From the front-end, we can access the back-end using a database language called SQL (Structured Query Language) by performing database queries and manipulations.

Fifth Generation Languages (5GL) are Visual Programming languages such as Visual Basic, Visual C++ and PC COBOL. They provide an environment called Integrated Development Environment (IDE), which includes all the necessary tools for program development and deployment. Some of the tools available in an IDE are: Editor, Screen Designer, Code Generator, Compiler and a Debugger.

Moreover, fifth generation languages use a visual or graphical development interface to design the User Interface (UI) and to generate the corresponding source code that can be usually compiled with a 3GL or 4GL language compiler. Microsoft Visual Studio 7, now known as Visual Studio.Net is an example of 5GL that allows programming languages such as COBOL, C++, Perl, SmallTalk, C#, Jscript, Visual Basic, Visual Foxpro and Java to share a single GUI.

Structured Programming and Object-Oriented Programming (OOP)

Third generation language such as C is also known as Procedural or Structured Programming language, because it separates data elements from the procedure (or action) that will be performed on them. They give more importance to actions (also called procedures) than the data handled by them. In this approach, application programs are divided into smaller programs known as functions. Most of the functions share the data globally.

On the other hand, languages like C++ and Java tie both data and functions (actions) into a single unit called an **Object**. An object consists of **data** and **functions** that operate on the data. Programming languages that are based on the object oriented concepts such as objects, encapsulation, data hiding, polymorphism and inheritance are called **Object Oriented languages**.

In Object Oriented Programming, any real world entity can be modeled as an object. The whole software is considered as a group of objects that work together to accomplish a particular task. During execution, objects interact with each other by sending messages and receiving responses. For instance, in a program that performs withdrawal from an account, a customer object may send a withdraw message to a bank account object in order to perform withdrawal.

Thus, OOP is defined as a method of programming in which programs are organized as co-operative collections of objects, each of which represents a real world entity. Any object that communicates with another object need not be aware of its internal workings but only its function signatures.

Chapter 2

STRUCTURED PROGRAMMING

Software development is a process of creating new software or modifying existing software for meeting the current requirements of its users. This process consists of various stages or phases in it.

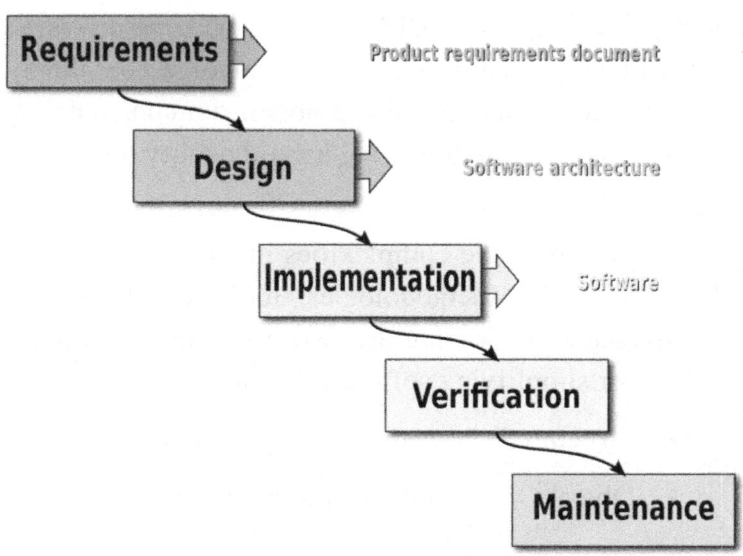

Software Development Life Cycle (SDLC)

Steps involved in Software Development process include the following:

1. Problem Definition (Analysis)

2. Program Design

3. Coding / Implementation

4. Testing and

5. Maintenance

A complete set of all these activities involved in developing software is known as Software Development Life Cycle (SDLC). This is because the same sequence of steps are to be followed whenever we develop new software from scratch or modifying existing software for up gradation.

Some small programs like creating a text editor (e.g., Notepad) can be done directly without following all the steps involved in SDLC. But, developing large programs like MS Word or MS Excel involve complexity in areas like understanding the problem domain, meeting the customer needs and delivering a good quality product in time.

To overcome the complexities involved in software development, many methodologies, tools and languages were introduced. Following are two major methodologies introduced for simplifying software development process:

> Structured (Procedural) Programming

> Object Oriented Programming (OOP)

Structured Programming:

In structured programming model, software designers tend to use Top-Down approach, in which the overall objective of the system is defined first. Then the system is divided into various sub tasks or sub modules. With this methodology, software development is done by writing a set of sub programs, called **functions** that can be integrated together to form a complex system.

In Structured programming, the primary focus is on functions. A function is a sub program that performs a specific task using the values given to it through input variables (called parameters) and then returns the result to its caller (main program). Each function consists of a set of program statements and some local variables. A function when invoked behaves as though its code is inserted at the point of its call. The communication between the **caller** (calling function) and the **callee** (called function) takes place through parameters. A typical program structure for structured approach is shown below:

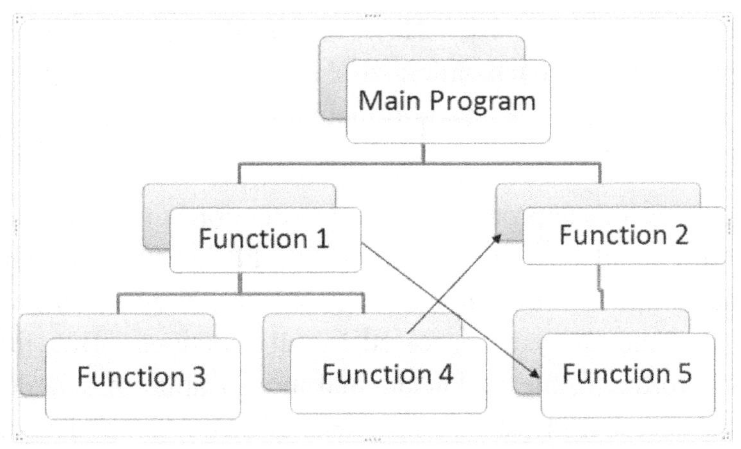

Structured Programming Model

At the time of function call, the control is transferred from the caller to the first statement of the callee (the function itself). All the statements in the function body are executed and then the control is transferred back to the caller to resume the execution of other statements.

Some characteristics exhibited by Structured (also called Procedural-oriented) programming are:

→ Emphasis is on doing things (algorithms)

→ Large programs are divided into smaller programs called functions.

→ Most of the functions share global data.

→ Data move openly around the system from function to function and

→ Employs Top-down approach in program design

Limitations of Structured Programming:

Structured programming was a powerful tool that enables programmers to write moderately complex programs fairly easily. However, as the programs grew larger, this approach failed to show the desired results in terms of bug-free, easy-to-maintain and reusability of programs.

In this approach, very little attention is given to data used by the function. And, in a multi-function program, many important data items are placed in the global scope, so that they may be accessed by all functions. But, this leads to the problem of accidental modification of data due to its access from various functions of the program. Hence, in a large program it is difficult to keep track of the data items having global scope. The following picture depicts the relationship of data and functions in structured (or) procedural programming.

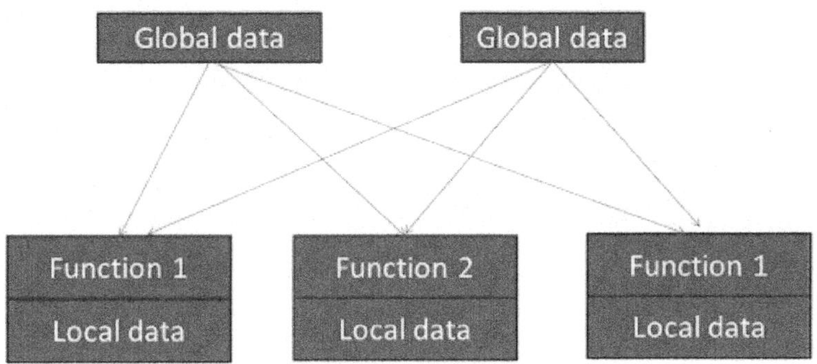

Relationship of data and functions in Structured programming

Another serious drawback with the procedural approach is that it does not model the real world entities to the elements in a program in a one-to-one manner. This is because the functions are action-oriented and they do not really correspond to the elements of the problem.

Object Oriented Programming - Defined:

Object Oriented Programming is centered on new concepts such as objects, classes, polymorphism, and inheritance. OOP is defined as follows: *It is a method of programming in which programs are organized as co-operative collections of objects, each of which represents an instance of some class and whose classes are all members of a hierarchy of classes united through the property called inheritance.*

Chapter 3

PLANNING A COMPUTER PROGRAM
(Part I)

Planning a computer program is nothing but planning the logic of the program. In order to produce a correct and effective computer program, the logic of the program has to be planned first. Without having the logic, a programmer can't write the program well.

In a computer program, all the instructions must be written in a proper sequence. When the order is not correct or some of the instructions are left out, the computer will calculate a wrong answer. To ensure the correct order and the appropriateness of the computer instructions, a program must be planned first. Planning a computer program is done with the help of planning tools and techniques, which include Algorithm, Flowchart and Pseudo code.

A sequence of instructions is called an **algorithm**. Writing algorithm is a fundamental part of computing. **Flowcharts** and **Pseudo code** are the two commonly used tools for designing the program logic (also called algorithm). Generally, flowcharts work well for small problems but Pseudo code is used for larger problems.

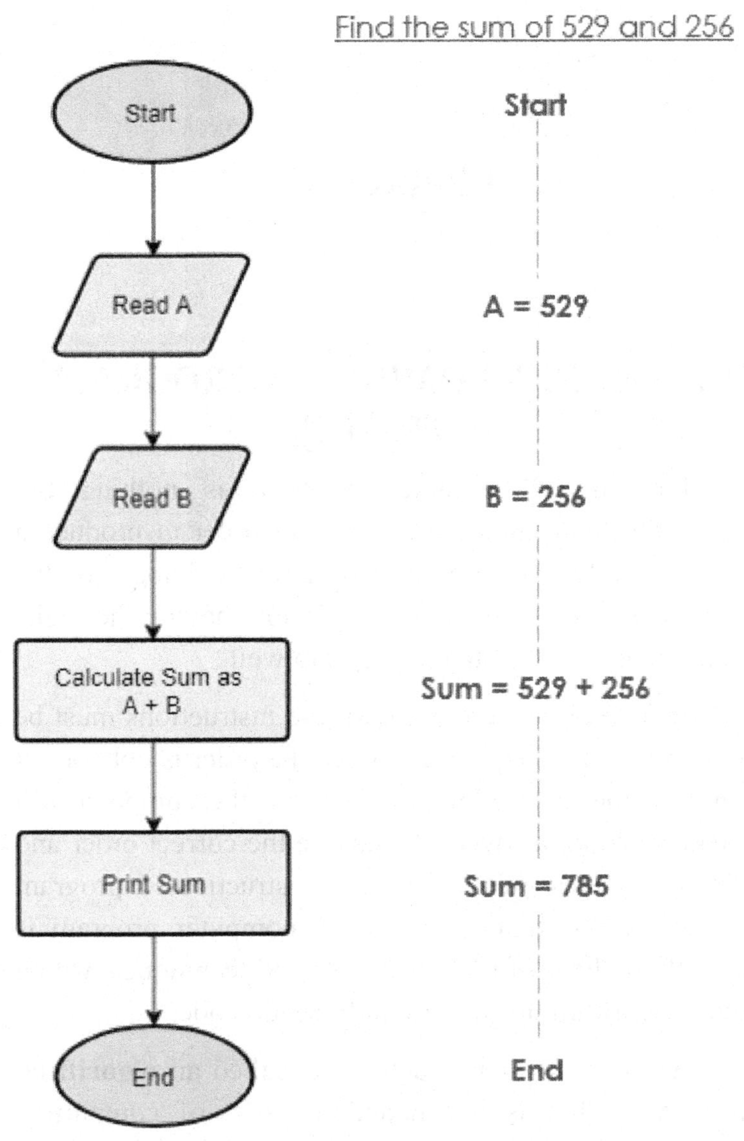

Planning a Program using Flowchart

20

Using Algorithm:

The term algorithm refers to the logic of the program. An algorithm is defined as a step-by-step description of how to arrive at the solution of a given problem. Algorithm contains a set of instructions that must be executed in a specified sequence to produce a desired result. The characteristics of a good algorithm are listed below:

1. Each and every instruction should be precise and unambiguous.

2. Each instruction should be designed in such a way that it can be performed in a finite time.

3. Not a single instruction should be repeated infinitely, i.e., there should be an end for an algorithm both logically and physically.

4. After the termination of an execution, the user must be able to get the desired output.

The following are three ways in which an algorithm can be represented:

- ❖ As Programs

- ❖ As Flowcharts

- ❖ As Pseudo codes

The first one is the language representation of an algorithm that can be compiled and executed by a computer to produce an expected output. When a high-level language is used for representing an algorithm, it becomes a computer program. The syntax and semantics of that particular programming language must be followed to write the program in it.

Normally an algorithm is written in simple and plain English. No rules and regulations are formed for writing an algorithm except some characteristics, which qualify a set of instructions to be an algorithm. To represent an algorithm pictorially a flowchart is used.

Using Flowchart:

A flowchart is a pictorial representation of an algorithm. Programmers often use it as a visual tool for organizing the sequence of steps necessary to solve a problem. The process of drawing a flowchart for an algorithm is often referred to as **flowcharting**. Some of the common symbols used in flowcharts are shown below.

Flowchart Symbols

Symbol	Meaning
	Start/Stop
	Process
	Input/Output
	Decision/Branching
	Connector
	Flow
	Manual Input
	Predefined Process

Symbols used in a Flowchart

A set of symbols is provided for drawing a flowchart and to represent different operations to be executed by a computer. The symbols used in a flowchart are connected together using arrow headed solid lines to indicate the sequence in which the instructions must be evaluated. Flowcharting is a task that must be done after writing the algorithm for a computer program. It is a pictorial representation of a program.

With flowcharting, essential steps of an algorithm are shown using the shapes called flowchart symbols. The flow of data between steps is indicated by arrows, or flow lines.

Average of 3 Numbers - sequence

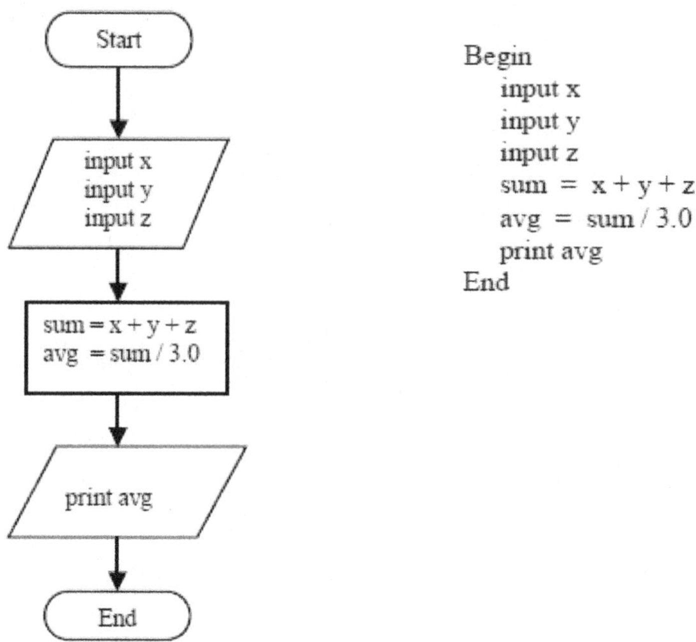

Flowchart & Its Corresponding Pseudo Code

The flowchart shown above is for getting three values as input, and to compute the sum and average of those numbers given as input. The average value has to be displayed as output to the user.

Chapter 4

PLANNING A COMPUTER PROGRAM (Part II)

The Pseudo code describes the essential steps to be taken in a program just like a flowchart, but without the graphical enhancements.

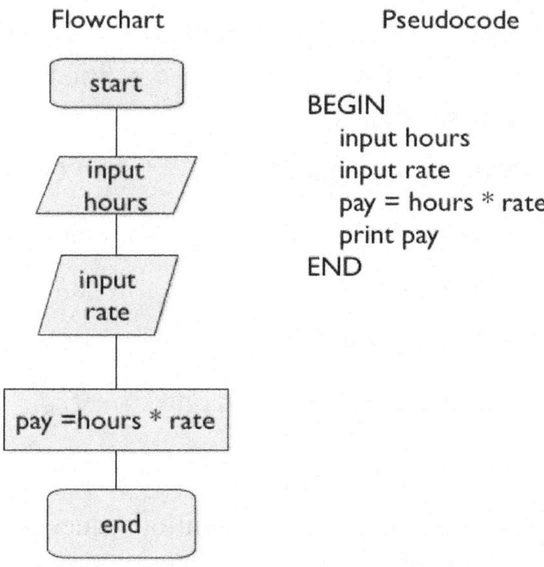

Two Different Representation of a Program

Decision Making (Switching logic):

Switching logic consists of two components - a condition and a *goto* command that gets executed depending on the result of the condition test. The condition is formed using one of the six mathematical relations symbolized in the table below:

Symbol	Meaning
==	Equals
!=	Not Equal
<	Less than
<=	Less than or equal to
>	Greater than
>=	Greater than or equal to

In practice, the computer is presented not with a true/false statement, but with a question that results either in "Yes" or "No" answer. For example if A = 10, B = 20, K = 5, and SALES = 10000, then the conditions and their results are tabulated below:

Condition (Question)	"Answer"
Is A == B?	No
Is B > A?	Yes
Is K <= 25?	Yes
Is SALES >= $5000.00?	Yes

While evaluating each condition (question) given above, the computer will take a different course of action depending on the answer it obtains.

In general, a step in an algorithm that leads to more than one possible continuation is called a decision. In flowcharting, the diamond-shaped symbol is used to indicate a decision. The question is placed inside the symbol, and each alternative answer to the question is used to label the exit arrow which leads to the appropriate next step of the algorithm. The decision symbol is the only symbol that may have more than one exit.

The below example is a flowchart for a program that reads two numbers and displays the bigger and the smaller number between those two numbers :

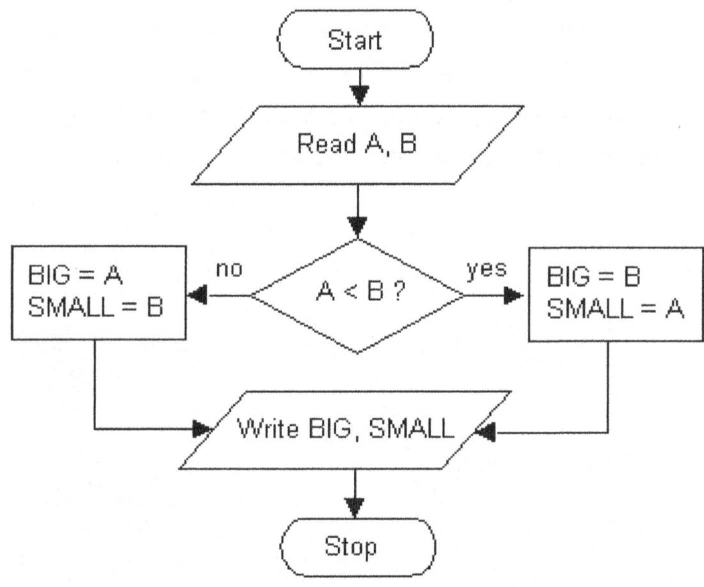

The equivalent Pseudo code of the above flowchart is shown below. Note that while writing the Pseudo code, indentation is used to show the steps to follow when a condition (decision) is true:

Read A, B
If A is less than B

$$BIG = B$$
$$SMALL = A$$

else

$$BIG = A$$
$$SMALL = B$$

Write (Display) BIG, SMALL

Looping Process:

Most programs involve repeating a series of instructions over and over until some event occurs. This repetitive operation is also known as looping or iterative process. Iteration is a repetitive process in which the program must count the number of times a certain operation occurs. For example, if we wish to read ten numbers and compute the average, we need a loop to count the number of times we have read the input.

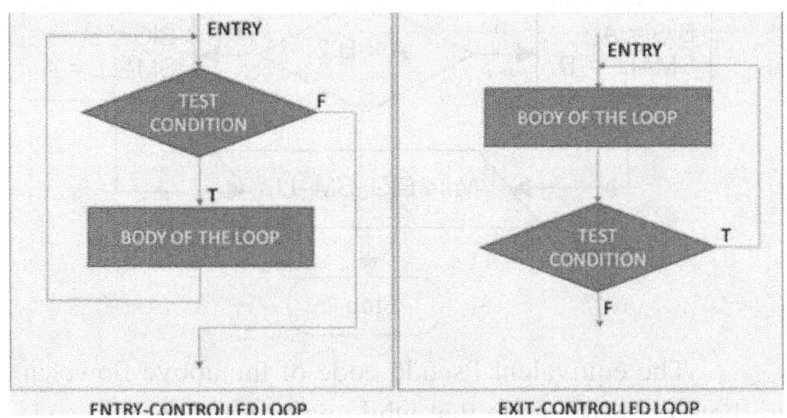

Two Types of Looping Structure

Among the flowcharts shown above, the one at the left represents an entry controlled loop, where as the flowchart at the right represent an exit-controlled loop. Entry controlled loop check the condition first and then

28

executes the loop, if the condition evaluates to true. On the other hand, exit controlled loop executes the body of the loop at least once whether the condition is true or false. Only at the end of the first iteration, the condition is evaluated.

In many cases we do not know how many times we want to do something. The number of iterations often dependent on the data provided to the program at runtime. In that case, we can go for while count loop which iterates 'n' times based on value of a variable.

Here is a problem that needs iteration: Read *n* numbers from the user and compute the average of all the given numbers. Here, we don't know how many numbers are to be read, but will read numbers until there are no more. Two alternative solutions are there for this kind of problem:

Pre-test loop:

set average to zero
set count to zero
set total to zero
read number
while (not end-of-data)
    increment count by 1
    total = total + number
    read number
if (count > 0) then
    average = total / count
display average

Post-test loop:

set count to zero
set total to zero
set average to zero
do

> *read a number*
> *increment count by 1*
> *total = total + number*

while (not end-of-data)
if (count > 0) then

> *average = total / count*

display average

The above two versions of pseudo code assume that the computer will tell the program when there are no more numbers in the input. This is called an **end-of-data** or **end-of-file** test.

There is an important difference between the pre-test and post-test loops. The pre-test version will not work if there is no input given by the user, whereas the post-test version executes the body of the code at least once.

Chapter 5

INTRODUCTION TO 'C' LANGUAGE

'C' is a structured, high-level, machine independent language. The early version of 'C' developed during 1970s is known as 'Traditional C'. Then, in the year 1989, 'ANSI C' was written to meet the standards set by the American National Standards Institute (ANSI) to become a standard structured programming language.

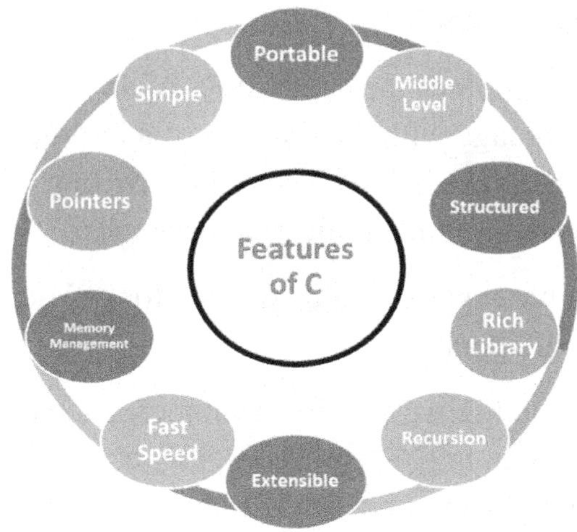

Some of the Features of C Language

Evolution of C

In the early 1960s, the language ALGOL was introduced. It was the first structured programming language. In 1967, Martin Richards developed a language called BCPL (Basic Combined Programming Language) primarily for writing system software. In 1970, Ken Thompson created another language called 'B' based on many features of BCPL.

The language 'B' was used for creating the early versions of UNIX OS. Finally, the language 'C' was developed based on many concepts of its predecessors by Dennis Ritchie at Bell Laboratories in 1972. The later versions of UNIX were coded almost entirely in C.

Characteristics of C

'C' language became very popular because of its special features as listed below:

1. It provides a rich set of built-in-functions and operators using which complex programs can be easily written.

2. It combines the capabilities of an assembly language with the features of a high-level language. Therefore it is well suited for writing both system software and application packages.

3. It has a variety of data types for efficient storage and operation.

4. It is highly portable. That means the programs written in C for one computer can run on another with little or no modification.

5. It promotes modularity in writing software by allowing the programs to be written as modules or sub programs. The name given for a sub program is 'Function'.

Structure of 'C' Program

The general basic structure of a C program is shown in the figure below. Program execution begins with the body of the function *main()*, which is enclosed within curly braces: "{" and "}". Function *main()* may contain both local variable declarations as well as one or more executable statements. The function *main()* can be preceded by other sections that include documentation, preprocessor statements and global declarations.

<table>
<tr><td colspan="2">Documentation section</td></tr>
<tr><td colspan="2">Link section</td></tr>
<tr><td colspan="2">Definition section</td></tr>
<tr><td colspan="2">Global declaration section</td></tr>
<tr><td colspan="2">main () Function section
{
    <table><tr><td>Declaration part</td></tr><tr><td>Executable part</td></tr></table>
}</td></tr>
<tr><td>Subprogram section
<table><tr><td>Function 1</td></tr><tr><td>Function 2</td></tr><tr><td>…………..</td></tr><tr><td>………….</td></tr><tr><td>Function n</td></tr></table></td><td>(User defined functions)</td></tr>
</table>

Basic Structure of a C Program

Documentation Section

The documentation section consists of a set of comment lines that can contain the name of the program, the author name and other information, which the programmer would like to use later.

Preprocessor Statements

The preprocessor statements begin with # symbol and are also called the **preprocessor directive**. These statements instruct the compiler to perform certain operations such as including header files or assigning values to constants (called symbolic constants) before starting the compilation process. Some of the preprocessor statements are listed below.

Preprocessor directive	
File inclusion directive	#include
Macro substitution directive	#define
Undefine symbol directive	#undef
Conditional directive	#if , #elif , #else , #endif , #ifdef , #ifndef
Miscellaneous directive	#pragma , #line , #error
Operator in preprocessor	# , ##, define( )

```
# include <stdio.h>   ⎫
# include <math.h>    ⎪
                      ⎬ header files
# include <stdlib.h>  ⎪
# include <CONIO.h>   ⎭

# define P L 3.1412.  ⎫
# define TRVE 1       ⎬ Symbolic constants
# define FALSE Ø      ⎭
```

Preprocessor Directives and their Usage in C

Global Declaration Section

The variables/functions that are declared prior to function *main()*, i.e., in the global declaration section are called **global variables/functions**. The global variables can be accessed by all the user defined functions including function *main()*.

The main ( ) function

Each and Every C program should contain only one *main()* function. Program execution starts with function *main()*. No C program can be written and executed without function *main()*. The *main()* function is generally written using small (lowercase) letters. It can be written using one or more executable statements, user defined functions or library functions.

Braces

The statements within function *main()* should be enclosed with in a pair of curly braces ({, }). The left brace indicates the beginning and the right brace indicates the end of the function *main()*. Here are some other usages of curly braces:

- To indicate the beginning and end of user-defined functions.

- To enclose compound statements in a program.

Local Declarations

The variable declaration is the first part of every C function that includes function *main()*. Variables declared within a function are called **local variables**. Here is an example of declaring local variables in function *main()*:

```
main() {

        int sum = 0;

        int x;

        float y;

}
```

In this example, the variables *sum* and *x* are declared as variables of type *integer*. Hence, they can be used for storing only integers throughout the program. Moreover the variable *sum* is initialized to zero at the time of declaration, i.e., its initial value is 0. There is one more variable named *y* that has been declared as a variable of type **float** for holding a floating point value within function *main()*.

Program statements

Statements are the sequence of instructions given in a program for performing certain operation using computer. They give instruction to the computer to perform a specific task (operation). An instruction is given using anyone of the following statements:

1. Input / Output statement

2. Assignment statement

3. Conditional Control statement

4. Comments that are enclosed within /* and */

The comments are not compiled and executed by the compiler. Except comments all other statements are compiled and executed by the computer at run time. They must all end with a semicolon.

User defined functions

User defined functions are **subprograms** written for performing a specific operation within a C program. Each subprogram contains a set of statements for performing a specific task. They are defined outside the function *main()*, and are placed either before or after the *main()* function. Here is a simple C program with function *main()* that will display a welcome message to the user:

```
#include <stdio.h>
main()
{
        printf("Welcome to the world of C\n");
}
```

Chapter 6

FUNDAMENTAL ELEMENTS OF C

Character sets are the basic building blocks of any programming language. In C, the character set consists of upper and lower case alphabets, digits, special characters and white spaces. The alphabets and digits constitute the alphanumeric set.

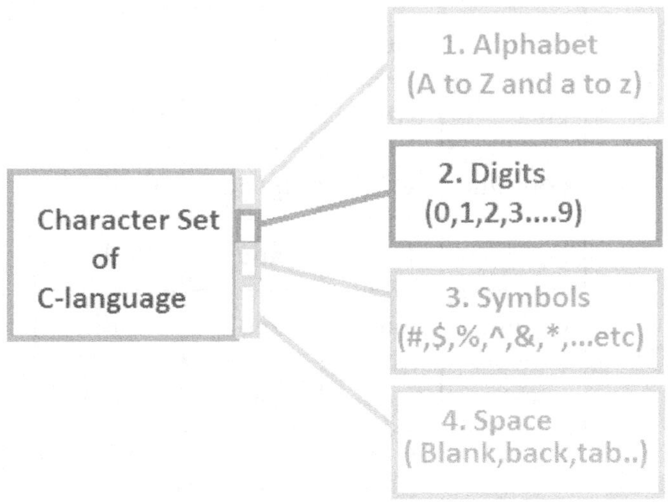

C Language Character Set

The smallest individual units in a program are known as **tokens**. Tokens are formed using one or more characters from the character set. A C program is written using one or more tokens and white spaces. C has five types of tokens namely: Keywords, Identifiers, Constants, Operators and Terminals.

Keywords

Keywords are special words, which are predefined in a language for a specific purpose in a program. They are explicitly reserved identifiers that can't be used as names for the program variables or user-defined data types and functions. Compiler knows the meaning of these words. All keywords are written in lowercase. Here is list of all keywords in C:

auto	double	int	struct
break	else	long	switch
case	enum	register	typedef
char	extern	return	Union
continue	for	signed	Void
do	if	static	While
default	goto	sizeof	volatile
const	float	short	unsigned

List of All Keywords in C

Identifiers

Identifiers are names given by the user for the programming elements such as variables, symbolic constants, functions, arrays and classes. Each language has its own rules for naming these identifiers. The following points must be noted while forming an identifier in C:

i.   Identifiers are formed using alphabets, digits and underscore characters.

ii. Every identifier must begin with an alphabet or underscore character.

iii. The maximum number of characters used for forming an identifier must not exceed 31.

iv. Identifiers are case sensitive, i.e. 'number' and 'Number' are two different identifiers. Similarly, variables names - rate, Rate, and RATE are treated as different identifiers.

v.   Identifier can't start with digit. i.e. '9number' is invalid identifier

Below are some valid identifier names.

- *number*

- *_money*

- *_student_*

- *car1234*

- *home321_*

It is a general practice to use lower and mixed case letters for identifiers. But keywords are always in lowercase letters.

Few Examples of Keywords and Identifiers:

int number;

In this line of code, we have declared the variable 'number' of type integer. 'int' is a keyword and 'number' is identifier.

long value;

Here, we have declared the variable 'value' of type long integer. 'long' is a keyword and 'value' is identifier.

char ch10;

Here, we have declared the variable 'ch10' of type character. 'char' is a keyword and 'ch10' is identifier.

Constants

Constants are values that never change during the execution of a program. For instance, the value 10 is an integer constant, 'A' is a character constant and "C Programming" is a string constant.

When constants are named using identifiers, they become **Symbolic Constants**. Symbolic constants are named constants that can be referred later in a program using the symbol used for their definition.

Variables

Variables can be considered as value container that will store value assigned to the variable. So if we want to keep some value preserved and want to use it later, we have to make use of variable in a C program.

A variable is an entity whose value can be changed during program execution and is known to a program by a name. A variable can hold only one value at a time during program execution.

A variable must be declared first before using it in a program. By declaring a variable, we reserve memory required for data storage and associate the memory with a symbolic name. The syntax for defining a variable is:

<datatype> <variable_1>, <variable_2>, <variable_3>......, <variable_N>;

where,

1. The data type can be any primitive or user-defined data type such as *int, float, double* and so on

2. Variable names can be any valid C identifier except reserved words.

Rules for declaring a variable are:

Variable name is an identifier so all rules of identifier is applied to variable name as well.

- Variable name can formed using alpha numeric characters (a-z, A-Z, 0-9) and underscore (_) characters

- Variable name can't start with digit. So '9mark' is an invalid variable name.

- Variable name is case sensitive. So 'number' and 'Number' are two different variables

Data Types in C

Data types are keywords that specify three things about an identifier called variable. They are as follows:

1. Type of data to be stored in a variable

2. Size of memory location required for storing the data and

3. The range of values a variable can hold

Data types are used in a program to declare variables. By declaring variables, we determine the set of values a variable can store and the various operations that can be performed on it. Following are the three major classifications of data types in C:

> Primary (fundamental) data type

> Derived data types and

> User-defined data type

Here are some examples of Variable Declaration:

int number;

Here 'int' is a data type and 'number' is variable name. 'number' is variable of type integer.

long marks, total;

Here 'long' is a data type and 'marks' and 'total' are variables 'marks' and 'total' are variables of type long integer.

char ch10;

Here 'char' is data type and 'ch10' is a variable name. 'ch10' is a variable of type character.

SECTION II

Writing Simple Programs in C

This section introduces the basic concepts of C Programming, which include the following:

Primitive Data Types in C

Creating User Defined Data Types

Operators and Expressions in C

Using Arithmetic, Relational & Logical Operators

Conditional Control Flow using if…else

Using Switch Statement for Branching

Unconditional GoTo Statement

Chapter 7

PRIMITIVE DATA TYPES IN C

Data type is a keyword that tells compiler what kind of variable is to be declared in a program. It dictates the compiler to reserve memory for variables.

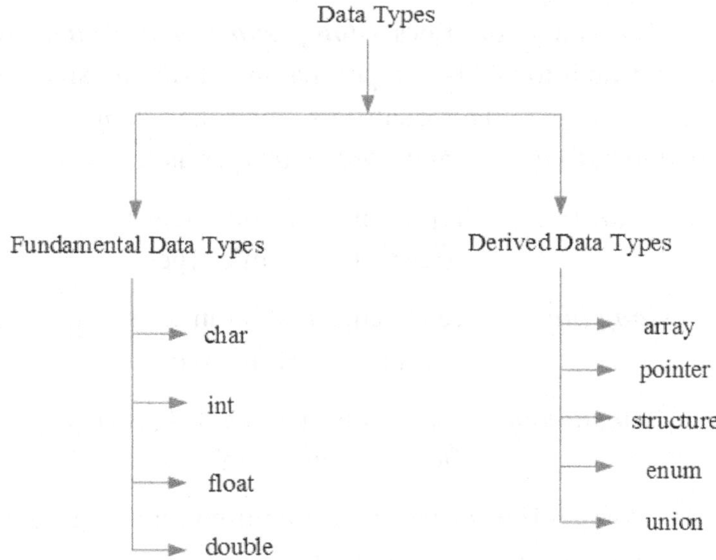

Classification of Data Types in C

C supports five basic (or fundamentals) data types namely *char, int, float, double and void.*

char represents a single byte that can hold one character. It is used to store single character (e.g. 'A', 'c', '$', '+', 'D')

int represents an integer. It is used to store whole numbers (e.g. 1, 100, 500, 2343, 45666)

float represents a single precision floating point number. It can be used to store real numbers (e.g. 2.3, 5.3, 66.44, 544.5)

double represents a double precision floating point number. It can be used to store real number with high precision of fractional part (e.g 2.44445453, 5.4445453543, 4.45353453453, 45.453534534534)

void represents no value. It is used to represent that it has no value. Generally used for mentioning function return type when function has nothing to return.

By using **qualifiers** - *long, short* or *unsigned*, we can have additional data types having different size and range of values. The qualifiers *short* and *long* can be applied to both *integer* and *float* data types as follows:

short int:	represents a 16 bit integer irrespective of m/c types
long int:	represents a 32 bit integer irrespective of m/c types
long double:	represents an extended precision floating point number

The qualifier *unsigned* can be used with data types: *int* and *char*, in order to increase their maximum range of values twice.

The qualifier *unsigned* restricts the user from storing negative values in its variables by setting the minimum range to 0. Therefore, the range of values for unsigned variables is 0 to a maximum value, which varies from data type to data type.

Integer Data Type

An integer is a whole number without any fraction. For instance, 100 is an integer that represents the age of a person. The following table lists out the range of values and bytes used for various types of integer and float:

Variable Type	Bytes Used	Range
short int	1	-128 to 127
unsigned short int	1	0 to 255
int	2	-32,768 to 32,767
unsigned int	2	0 to 65,535
long int	4	-2,147,483,648 to 2,147,483,647
unsigned long int	4	0 to 4,294,967,295
float	4	-3.4E-38 to 3.4E+38
double	8	-1.7E-308 to 1.7E+308

Data types and their Storage Requirement

Generally, integer occupies two bytes of memory location to store the range of values from -32768 to 32767. If we want to increase the range of values to be stored in an integer variable, we need to declare it as an unsigned integer using the qualifier *'unsigned'* as prefix:

unsigned *integer age*;

The variable *age* of type *unsigned integer* can store only a positive number and in the range of 0 to 65355. Thus, an **unsigned integer** uses only 2 bytes of memory for its storage, whereas a **long integer** takes four bytes of memory to store a number in the range of -2,147,483,648 to 2,147,483,647.

Real Data Type

A real number is a number having two parts: integer part and decimal part. The integer part has a whole number, which is followed by dot and a fractional number. A fraction is a value which is less than 1.

A real number can be represented in fraction or using scientific notation. There are two fundamental data types in C for declaring variables that can hold real data: **float** and **double**. A variable declared as *float* is assigned four bytes of memory to store a real number.

To increase the range of values to be stored in a real variable, declare it using the data type *double*. A variable of type *double* will occupy eight bytes of memory to store more range of values than that of a floating point variable. The following are some of the examples for declaring variables using fundamental data types:

int age;

float amount;

double per_marks;

Character Data Type

A character variable can hold a single character, using 8 bits of memory cells. A character is represented externally in a program as a symbol enclosed in a pair of single quotes. For instance,

char *alpha = 'R';*

assigns the label R to the variable *alpha*. Actually, characters are represented in memory by a number, called **code** (ASCII code). For example, the code for letter A is 65, for B is 66 and so on.

A string in C is a sequence of characters stored in consecutive memory locations followed by a **null** character. The null character is assigned the ASCII code 0 and is called **end-of-string marker.** In C, string constants are enclosed in double quotes as follows:

"Hello, World!"

Chapter 8

USER DEFINED DATA TYPES IN C

User defined data type is built upon basic type. **Enumerated data type** is a user defined type, which specifies a finite set of named values called **enumerated constants.**

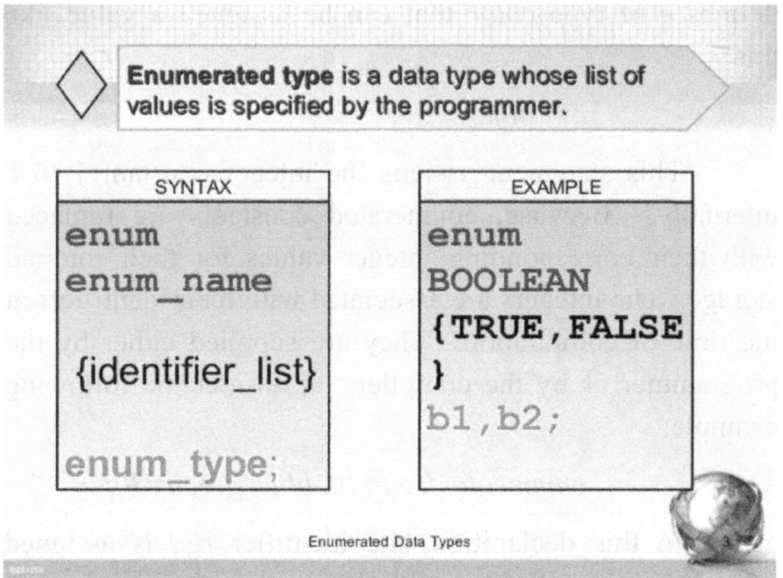

Defining and Using Enumerated Data Type in C

Like characters, enumerated constants are assigned integer values for their internal storage. Following is an example for declaring enumerated data type with enumerated constants:

enum color{red, blue, green};

The above statement defines *color* as a new data type of type *enum* with values specified as *red*, *blue* and *green*. Each of these identifiers (called **enumerated symbols**) is assigned a constant such as 0, 1 and 2 respectively.

After the declaration, the enumerated data type *color* can be used for declaring variables just like a fundamental data type. A variable of type *color* can have any one of three values (*red*, *blue*, and *green*) at any point of time. For example, the statement:

color c;

defines *c* of type *color* that can be assigned a value like this:

c = blue;

This statement assigns the integer constant 1 to *c* internally. Because, enumerated constants are replaced with their corresponding integer values for their internal storage. The integers are associated with their identifiers at the time of compilation. They are supplied either by the programmer or by the compiler. Consider the following example:

enum color{red=10, blue, green=30};

In this declaration, the identifier *red* is assigned with the integer 10, blue with the next consecutive integer 11, and green with 30. If the integer value is not given explicitly to the first enumerated constant, it is taken as 0. Now, the assignment statement:

c = green;

assigns the value 30 to c. Suppose, two enumerated constants are assigned with the same value as follows:

enum weather{hot, warm=0, cold, wet};

Then the constants *hot* and *warm* can be interchangeably used in order to assign the value 0, because both of them are assigned with value 0.

Use only enumerated constants with enumerated variables. If we assign any other value other than the one specified in the declaration, the compiler will give a warning message in order to avoid any invalid assignment. Enumeration is a convenient way to associate constant integers with meaningful names. Using enumerated constants in a program makes it easier to read and change the code at a later date.

Array

Array is a special variable or identifier in C and is defined using any one of the basic data types (*char*, *int*, *float*, or *double*) for storing more than one (multiple) values of that particular data type at a time. For example,

int nums[10]; // Here 'nums' is an array of 10 elements of integer kind.

char name[12]; // Here 'name' is an array of 12 elements of character kind.

Structure Data type

Structure data type is a derived data type in C that can store different type of data in a single variable at any point of time. It is used to group variables (also called members) of different data type into a single entity called structure. Thus, the variables of type *structure* can hold a set of values that belongs to a record. For example,

struct {

    int item_id,

    float item_value

} item;

// Here 'item' is a structure variable having two members.

// 'item_id' is a member of integer type.

// 'item_value' is a member of floating type.

Chapter 9

OPERATORS AND EXPRESSIONS

Operators are special characters or symbols, which instruct the compiler to perform certain operation on one or more operands. Operands are data items such as variables or literals that the operators act upon.

Arithmetic Operator

Operator	Description
*	multiplication
/	division
%	modulo
+	addition
-	subtraction

Relational Operator

Oerator	Description
<	less than
>	greater than
>=	greater than or equal
==	equal to
!=	not equal

Logical Operator

Operator	Description
!	NOT
&&	AND
||	OR

Bitwise Operators

Operator	Description
~	One's complement
<<	Left shift
>>	Right shift
&	Bitwise AND
^	Bitwise XOR

Classification of Operators in C

Operators in C are used to perform various operations on variables or data to generate new result. For example, to add two numbers we will use '+' operator.

Some operators operate on a single operand and they are called **unary operators**. But, most operators require two operands to perform their operation and hence they are called **binary operators**. For example,

-5   *++i*   *--i*

are expressions that use unary operators (+ and -), whereas

a+5

is an expression using binary operator +.

C operators are classified into various categories based on their type of operation they perform on the operands. They are namely Arithmetic operators, Relational operators, Logical operators, Assignment operators and Bitwise operators.

What is Expression?

An expression is a combination of variables, constants and operators written according to the syntax of the language. Every expression used in a program evaluates to a value. This means, after execution, it results in some value of a valid data type that can be assigned to a variable. The following are some of the valid expressions:

a+20

*c+b*2*

total+20+c/3

The operands used in an expression may be of different data types. An expression with operands of different types is called **mixed-mode expression**. The following code illustrates this:

int a, c;

float d, e;

e = (a+c+d);

The above expression is a mixed-mode expression, which uses two integers and two floating-point variables.

Mixed-mode expressions use type casting (conversion) for some of its operands before it takes on its final value. Generally, the operands of smaller size are converted to operands of larger size to get the right output. This process of converting the type of one operand to another is called **casting**, and is done implicitly by the compiler for mixed-mode expressions.

In an expression, for instance, if one operand is of type *float* and the other is of type *int*, then the variable of type *int* will be converted to floating-point type. And the result of this operation will also be of type *float* in order to accommodate the resultant value.

Arithmetic Operators

Arithmetic operators are operators that operate on numerical data and result in a numerical value. They take operands of type *int*, *float* or *char*. A character is also considered as an integer, if it is used in an expression, and the integer equivalent of the character (an ASCII value) will be used for its evaluation.

There are five different arithmetic operators in C. They are: + (addition), - (subtraction), * (multiplication), / (division) and % (modulo division). The operators + and −

can act as unary as well as binary operators. When act on single operand, these operands specify the sign of the operand that follow them. The default sign for any number used in an expression is + (positive).

Among these two unary operators (+ and -), the negative sign (-) is used often. It is used to specify a negative number or to negate the value stored in a variable. For e.g., consider the following statements:

int x = 5;

y = -x;

These two lines of code assign the value 5 to x, and then negates. Therefore, the final value of y is -5. If x is assigned the value -5 (i.e., x = -5) in the above example, then the value of y will be 5.

Binary Arithmetic Operators

The operators + and – take two operands if they are used for performing addition or subtraction on numbers. Depending on the type of operands they operate on, they perform either integer or floating-point arithmetic operation. When both operands are integer, then integer arithmetic is performed, which always yield an integer result. For instance, x and y are integers with values 16 and 5, the arithmetic is done like this:

int x = 16, y = 5;

x + y = 21 and

x – y = 11

Not only + and -, but also other arithmetic operators operate on two operands. The **multiplication operator (*)** multiplies two numbers, whereas the **division operator (/)**

divides the first operand by the second operand and returns the quotient. There is another arithmetic operator named **modulo division** (%), which is also a division operator except that it returns the remainder as its result.

Floating-point Arithmetic

Floating-point arithmetic involves operands of type *float* or *double* with their values specified either in decimal or exponential notation. The result is also a floating-point number, but rounded off to the number of significant digits specified. All the binary operators except modulo division operate on floating point operands. The following statements illustrate the use of arithmetic operators:

$$flaot\ a = 14.0,\ b = 4.0;$$

$$p = a\ /\ b;$$

$$q = b\ /\ a;$$

$$r = a + b;$$

The above operations result in values 3.500000, 0.285714, and 18.00000 for *p, q* and *r* respectively.

In mixed-mode arithmetic, if either one of the operands is *real*, the resultant value is always real. For e.g.,

$$35\ /\ 5.0 = 7.0$$

Here, since 5.0 is a double constant, 35 is converted to a value of type double (35.0) and the result is also a double constant.

Precedence of Arithmetic Operators

Precedence determines the order of evaluating operators in an expression. Generally, operators are evaluated from left to right in an expression. While evaluating an expression, the following rules of precedence are applied on operators:

1. Operators within parenthesis are processed first. Within parenthesis operators are evaluated from left to right.

2. Operators having higher priorities, which include *, / and % are applied next.

3. Operators such as + and – (having lower priority) are applied last.

Hence, a complex expression formed using parenthesis and a set of arithmetic operators and operands may take two to three passes to complete the entire evaluation process. During the first pass, operators within the parenthesis are evaluated; then the operators with higher precedence and finally, the operators with lower precedence are processed.

Here is example of using arithmetic operators.

#include <stdio.h>

int main()

{

int num1, num2, sum, mul; // Declare variables 'num1', 'num2', 'sum', 'mul'

num1 = 2; // Assign 2 to variable 'num1'

num2 = 5; // Assign 5 to variable 'num2'

sum = num1 + num2; // Using '+' operator to add 'num1' and 'num2'

printf("%d\n", sum); // Display 'sum' on screen

```c
    mul = num1 * num2; // Using '*' operator to multiple 'num1' and 'num2'

    printf("%d", mul); // Display 'mul' on screen

    return 0;

}
```

Chapter 10

RELATIONAL AND LOGICAL OPERATORS

A relational operator is a kind of operator, which is used to make comparisons between two operands. All relational operators are binary operators and require two operands.

Operator	Use	Example
<	Less than	if (a<b)
<=	Less than or equal to	if (a<=b)
>	Greater than	if (a>b)
>=	Greater than or equal to	if (a>=b)
==	Equal	if (a==b)
!=	Not equal	if (a!=b)

Use of Relational Operators in C

In a relational expression, the relational operator compares its left hand side operand with its right hand side operand. The result of this comparison will be an integer (zero or non-zero value).

If the comparison evaluates to true, it is indicated by a non-zero value, otherwise 0 will be the result to indicate false.

Relational operators are used generally in a comparison statement like **if... else** in C. If the expression given in the conditional part of *if* statement evaluates to true, the statements written in *if* block executes, otherwise, the statements in the *else* part executes. The syntax of *if... else* statement is this:

if (condition)

statement (s)

else

statement (s)

In relational expressions, similar quantities are often compared for taking decisions. Based on the result of the expression evaluation, the control is transferred to execute the corresponding block of statement.

Logical Operators

Logical operators are operators used for the following two purposes:

> ➢ To combine two or more relational expression

> ➢ To negate the result of a logical expression from true to false or vice versa

There are three logical operators provided in C for forming complex logical expressions. They are given in the following table:

Operator	Meaning
&&	Logical AND
||	Logical OR
!	Logical NOT

Logical Operators in C

The first two logical operators (&& and ||) are binary and are used to combine two or more logical condition, where as the third operator – exclamation (!) is a unary operator and is used to negate a condition.

The logical AND (&&) takes two expressions, one at its left and one at its right and checks whether both are evaluated to true. The compiler will evaluate the expression at left first, and if it results in true, then only it will evaluate the expression at the right of the logical operator. If both expressions evaluate to true, the result will be true (a non-zero value) or else false (0).

The logical OR (||) does the comparison of two expressions, one at its left, another at its right, to know whether one of the expressions evaluate to true. If either or both of them results in true, it evaluates to a non-zero value indicating true, or else false (0).

Logical NOT

The ! (NOT) operator takes a single expression and evaluates to *true* if the expression is *false*, and evaluates to *false* if the expression is *true*. In other words, it just reverses the value of the expression. For example, the expression

$$!(x >= y)$$

is evaluated as $x < y$. Similarly, the expression

$$a == 0$$

is equivalent to *!a*. The expression *!a* evaluates to true if the variable *a* holds zero, false otherwise.

Logical Operator Precedence

While evaluating the expression, the unary operator – negation (!) has the highest priority among the three, followed by the logical AND (&&) and then the logical OR (||). They are evaluated from left to right. The following program illustrates the use of logical expression to find whether a given year is leap or not:

```
#include <iostream.h>

void main()

{
        int year;
        printf("Enter any year :");
        scanf("%d",year);
        printf("%d", year);
        if( (year % 4 == 0  && year % 100 != 0) || (year % 400 == 0))
                printf("is a leap year");
        else
                printf("is not a leap year");
}
```

Chapter 11

USING ASSIGNMENT OPERATORS

An assignment operator is an equal sign (=) which evaluates the expression on the right and assigns the resultant value to the variable on the left.

Types of Assignment Operators

Using Assignment operator, we can do the following:

1. Initial values can be assigned to variables at the beginning of (a program) their usage in a program.

2. The result of an expression can be stored in a variable for later use.

The general form of the assignment statement is as follows:

variable-name = expression;

The expression can be a constant, variable name, or an expression (combination of variables, constants and operators). Here is an example assignment statement:

$a = c + d - 5;$

Combined Assignment Operators

Combined assignment operator is an assignment operator which is prefixed by an arithmetic operator like + or -. The following is a list of possible compound assignment operators:

$$+= \qquad -= \qquad /= \qquad \%=$$

$$\&= \qquad |= \qquad <<= \qquad >>=$$

Only binary operators can be combined with assignment operator to form a combined assignment operator. The syntax for compound assignment expression is as follows:

variable operator = expression / constant/ function;

These operators evaluate the expression on their right, and use the result to perform the corresponding operation on the variable at the left. Thus the statement:

variable operator = expression;

is equivalent to

variable = variable operator expression;

For example, the assignment statement

$$i\ {+}{=}\ 10;$$

is evaluated as $i = i + 10;$

The Assignment Anywhere Side Effect

C allows the use of assignment statements almost anywhere. We can even put assignment statements inside another assignment statement.

```
/* Please don't program like this */

average = total_value / (number_entries = last - first);
```

This is the same as saying:

```
/* Please program like this */

number_entries = last - first;

average = total_value / number_entries;
```

C also allows us to put an assignment in the while conditional.

```
/* Please don't program like this */

while ((current_number = last_number +
old_number) < 100)

        printf("Term %d\n", current_number);
```

The above piece of code is clear if it is written as the code given below. Notice how much clearer the logic is in the following?

```
/* Please program like this */

while (1)

{

current_number = last_number + old_number;
```

```c
if (current_number >= 100)
    break;
    printf("Term %d\n", current_number);
}
```



```c
if (current_number >= 100)
    break;
```

```c
}
```

Chapter 12

CONTROL FLOW STATEMENT IN C

Statements are the instructions to be followed while executing a program. They instruct a computer to perform a computation, store values in memory or call functions to accomplish a particular task. At runtime, statements are executed in sequence, one after another.

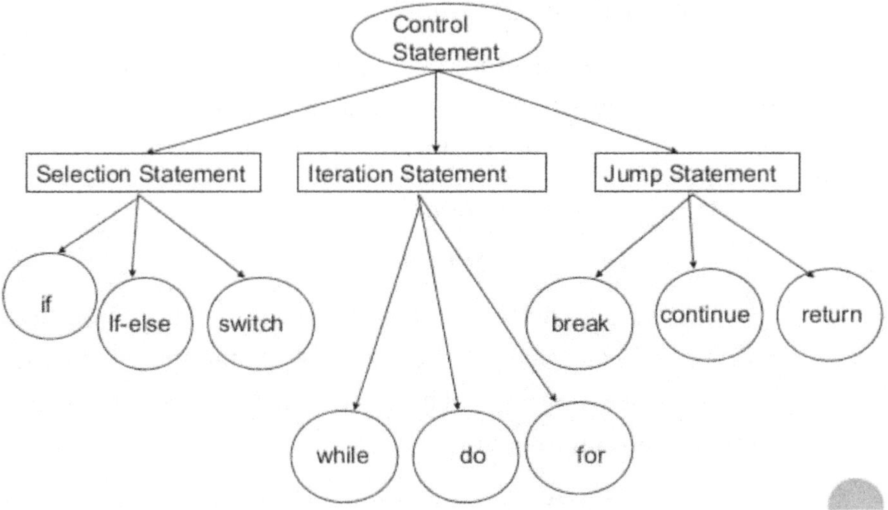

Control Flow Statements in C

We can, however, modify the sequence of execution by using *control flow statement* that allows a statement or group of statements to be executed only if some condition is met. Some control flow statements allow certain operations perform over and over again by forming a *loop*.

A somewhat different kind of control flow happens when we call a function: execution of the caller is suspended while the called function proceeds.

In general, control statements allow a programmer to specify the order in which the statements are to be executed. There are two types of control statements in any programming language, namely branching and looping.

Branching statements cause one section of code to be executed over the other based on the result of a conditional clause. Looping statements, on the other hand, are used to repeat a section of code a number of times or until some condition occurs.

The `if` statement

`if` statement allows a programmer to have control over the flow of execution of a program based on some condition. The general form of an `if` statement is:

if (condition)

statement;

If the condition is true (i.e., results in a non-zero value), the statement in the body of *if* statement will run, otherwise it won't run. The condition is formed using one of the relational operators.

There may be one or more statements in the body of *if* statement. If the body contains more than one statement, the statements are grouped by enclosing them within curly braces as in the following example:

```
if (total <= 0) {
    count++;
    printf("You owe nothing. \n");
}
```

For readability, the statements enclosed in {} are usually indented. This allows the programmer to easily see which statements are to be conditionally executed. As we will see later, mistakes in indentation can result in programs that are misleading and hard to read. An alternate form of the `if` statement:

```
if (condition)
    statement;          /* execute if condition is True */
else
    statement;          /* execute if condition is False */
```

Here is an example if..else statement:

```
if (total <= 0)
        printf("You owe nothing. \n");
else
        printf("You owe %d dollars. \n", amount);
```

In this example, if the condition is true (i.e., the variable *total* has a value less than 0), the *printf()* statement placed under *if* part will get executed, otherwise the *printf()* statement placed under *else* part will get executed.

The `if-else-if` Ladder

The if-else-if ladder is sometimes called the if-else-if staircase, because of its appearance. Its general form is:

if (expression)

> *statement;*

else

> *if (expression)*
>
> > *statement;*
>
> *else if(expression)*
>
> > *statement;*
>
> *else*
>
> > *statement;*

The conditions are evaluated from the top downward. As soon as a true condition is found, the statement associated with it will get executed and the rest of the ladder is bypassed. If none of the conditions are true, the statement in the final *else* will get executed. That is, if all other conditional tests fail, the last else statement will take care of the operation.

If the *final* else is not present, no action takes place if all other conditions are false. Although the indentation of the preceding if-else-if ladder is technically correct, it can lead to overly deep indentation. For this reason, the if-else-if ladder is generally indented like this:

if (expression)

> *statement;*

else if (expression)

> *statement;*

else if (expression)

statement;

else

statement;

The Nested ifs

A nested *if* is a kind of *if* statement that is the target of another *if* or *else* statement. Nested *if*s are very common in programming. In a nested *if*, an else statement is always connected to the nearest *if* statement within the same block as the *else* statement. For example,

if(i)

{

    if(j) statement 1;

    if(k) statement 2; / this if */*

    else statement 3; / is associated with this else */*

}

else statement 4; / associated with if(i) */*

In this example, the final else is not associated with *if(j)* because it is not in the same block. Rather, the final else is associated with *if(i)*. Similarly, the inner else is associated with *if(k)*, which is the nearest if.

The magic number program

Here is a program written using *if..else..if* ladder:

int main(void)

{

    int magic; / magic number */*
    int guess; / user's guess */*

```c
magic = rand(); /* generate the magic number */
printf("Guess the magic number: ");
scanf("%d", &guess);
if(guess == magic)
{
        printf("** Right ** ");
        printf("%d is the magic number", magic);
}
else if(guess > magic)
        printf("Wrong, too high");
else printf("Wrong, too low");
return 0;
}
```

The above C program will generate a random number every time it gets executed. It will prompt the user to enter a number that resembles the generated random number.

If the number entered by the user is same as that of the number generated by the program, the user is right in guessing the magic number generated by the computer. Otherwise, the program will compare the number entered by the user with that of the number generated by it and output the whether the difference is too high or too low.

Chapter 13

USE OF SWITCH & GOTO STATEMENT

The *switch* statement allows a programmer to select from multiple choices based on a set of fixed values for a given expression. It causes the control to be transferred to one of several statements (called sub statement) depending on the value of an expression, which must result in an integer.

The sub statement controlled by a switch is typically compound and hence they are enclosed within curly braces {}. Every sub statement must be associated with a case using a label, which consist of the keyword **case** followed by a constant expression and then a colon (:). The syntax of switch statement is as follows:

```
switch (expression)
{
case value1:
        statement1;
        break;          /* optional line */
case value2:
```

statement2;
break;   / optional line */*

....

....

....

default:
    default statement
    break;   / optional line */*

}

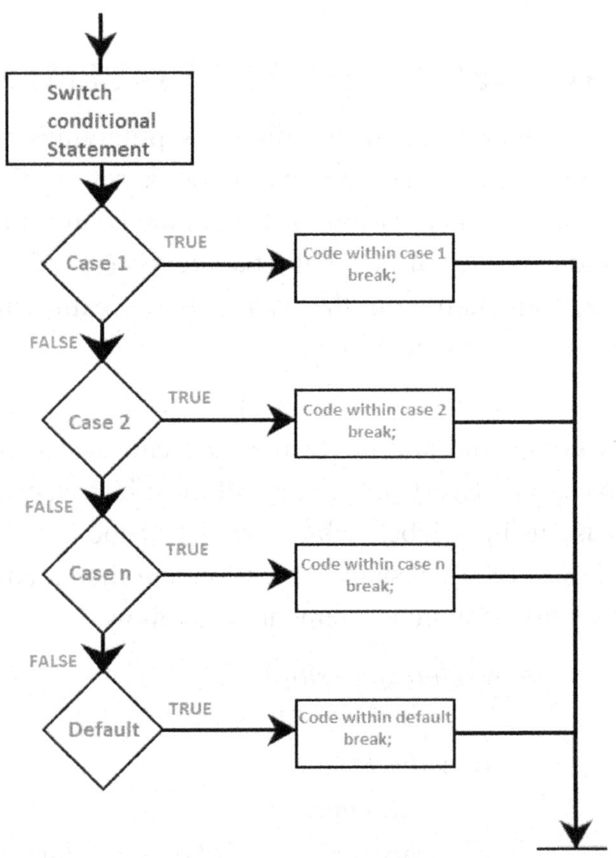

Flow Diagram of a Switch-Case Statement

No two of the case constants associated with the same switch may have the same value. There may be at most one **default** label associated with a switch. If none of the case labels are selected based on the expression given in the switch condition, then control will pass on to the default case. If there is no default case, execution resumes just beyond the entire construct.

break statement is used in a case block to cause the control to transfer to the statement following the closing brace for the switch. The *break* statement is not mandatory, but if it is not used at the end of every case section, the "fall through" will occur.

Switch statements can "fall through", when one case section has completed its execution, statements will continue to be executed downward until a break statement is encountered. Fall-through is useful in some circumstances, but is usually not desired.

Switches may be nested, i.e., a case or default label may contain another switch statement with in itself. Here is an example code for using *switch* statement in C:

```
#include <stdio.h>
main()
{
  int menu, numb1, numb2, total;
  printf("Enter any two numbers -->");
  scanf("%d %d", &numb1, &numb2 );
  printf("Enter your choice\n");
  printf("1=addition\n");
  printf("2=subtraction\n");
```

```c
scanf("%d", &menu );
switch( menu ) {
case 1: total = numb1 + numb2; break;
case 2: total = numb1 - numb2; break;
default: printf("Invalid option selected\n");
}
if( menu == 1 )
        printf("%d plus %d is %d\n", numb1,
numb2, total );
else if( menu == 2 )
        printf("%d minus %d is %d\n", numb1,
numb2, total );
}
```

<u>Sample Program Output:</u>

```
Enter any two numbers --> 37 23
Enter your choice
1=addition
2=subtraction
2
37 minus 23 is 14
```

Goto Statement

The ***goto*** is a unconditional branching statement used to transfer control of the program from one statement to another.

Syntax of ***goto*** statement is:

goto name1;

………… ……………

………… …………

………… …………

name1:
Statement;

where,

name1 mentioned identifies the place where the branch is to be made.

name1 is a valid variable name followed by a colon.

name1 is placed immediately before the statement where the control is to be transformed.

A program may contain several *goto* statements. The names mentioned in *goto* must be unique for branching.

Control can be transferred out of or within a compound statement and control can be transferred to the beginning of a compound statement. However the control cannot be transferred into a compound statement.

One must take care not to use too much of *goto* statements in their program or in other words use it only when needed. This is because C being a highly structured language one must take care not to use too much of these unconditional **goto** branching statements.

The *goto* statement is discouraged in C, because it alters the sequential flow of logic that is the characteristic of C language. This word is redundant in C and encourages poor programming style.

SECTION III

Using Advanced Concepts in C

This section explains some of the advanced programming concepts in C Programming, which include the following:

Iterative Process using While & For Loop

Defining User Defined Functions in C

Declaring and Using Pointers

Array for Storing Numeric Values

Character Array & Character Strings

Declaring and Using Structure for Storing Records

Chapter 14

ITERATIVE STATEMENTS IN C
(PART I)

In looping, a sequence of statements are executed until some condition is satisfied which is placed for termination of the loop.

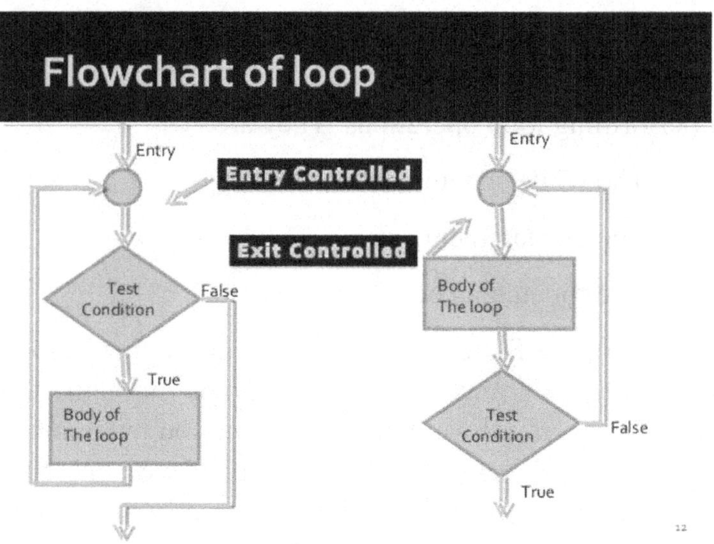

Flow Diagram of Loop Control Statement in C

A program loop consists of two segments, one is the body of the loop and the other known as the control statement. The control is tested always for execution of the body of the loop.

Depending on the position of the control statement in the loop, a control may be classified as the entry-controlled loop or as the exit-controlled loop. In the entry-controlled loop, first the conditions are tested and if satisfied then only body of loop is executed. In the exit-controlled, the test is made at the end of the body, so the body is executed unconditionally first time.

A looping process, in general, would involve the following four steps:

1. Setting and initialization of a counter.

2. Execution of the statements in the loop.

3. Test for a specified condition for execution of the loop.

4. Incrementing the counter.

The C language provides for three loop constructs for performing loop operations. They are:

i.   The while statement.

ii. The do statement.

iii. The for statement.

Looping Statements allow the program to repeat a section of code any number of times or until some condition occurs. If we don't have a limit on the number of times the loop is supposed to occur, or if we don't have a condition to satisfy, the loop will execute forever, something to avoid, usually.

The while Statement

This is one of the simplest looping structures. The basic format of the while statement is

> ***while*** *(test condition)*
> *{*
>
>   *body of the loop*
>
> *}*

The while is an entry-controlled loop statement. The test condition is evaluated and only if the condition is true the body is executed. After execution of the body, the test-condition is once again evaluated and if it is true, the body is executed once again.

This process of repeated execution of the body continues until the test-condition finally becomes false and the control is transferred out of the loop. On exit, the program continues with the statement immediately after the body of the loop. If the body contains only one statement, it is not necessary to put the braces, but placing them is a good programming practice.

Here is an Example for using a control loop:

```
........

.......

x = 10;              ------------- Initialization

while (x < 16)       ------------- Test condition

{

printf("%d",x);      ------------- body of the loop
x = x+1;

}

........
```

The above example shows a simple position where the test condition is evaluated first and since the test is satisfied the body is executed. This will continue exactly six times printing out 10 to 15. Finally when x becomes 16 then test fails & so the loop ends. The program continues with the statements after the loop.

This next program will compute all the fibonaci numbers that are less than 100.

```
#include <stdio.h>
int main(void)
{
        int old_number;         /* previous
Fibonacci number */
        int current_number;   /* current Fibonacci
number */
        int next_number;        /* next number in the
series */
        /* start things out */
        old_number = 1;
        current_number = 1;
        printf("1\n");             /* print first number
*/
        while (current_number < 100)
        {
                printf("%d\n", current_number);
                next_number = current_number +
old_number;
                old_number = current_number;
                current_number = next_number;
        }
```

return 0;

}

A Fibonacci series is generated by adding the previous two numbers to get the next number, so it looks like this:

0 1 1 2 3 5 8 13 21 34 ...

In mathematical terms, this is represented in a formula as:

fn = f(n-1) + f(n-2)

Mathematicians use this very terse style of naming variables. In the above program, the variables were renamed:

fn   => next_number

f(n-1) => current_number

f(n-2) => old_number

We want to loop until our current term is 100 or larger. The `while' loop: while (current_number < 100) will repeat our computation and printing until we reach this limit.

The `break' statement

Loops can be exited at any point through the use of a `break' statement. Suppose we want to add a series of numbers, but we don't know how many numbers are to be added together? We need some way of letting the program know we have reached the end of our list. In the next program, we use the number zero (0) to signal the end of the list:

#include <stdio.h>
int main(void)

```c
{
    char line[100];  /* line for data input */
    int total;  /* running total of numbers */
    int item;        /* next item to add to list */
    total = 0;
    while (1)
    {
        printf("Enter # to add\n");
        printf(" or 0 to stop: ");
        fgets(line, sizeof(line), stdin);
        sscanf(line, "%d", &item);
        if (item == 0)
            break;
        total += item;
        printf(Total: %d\n", total);
    }
    printf("Final total %d\n", total);
    return (0);
}
```

In the above program, because the `while' statement is written as:

```c
while (1)
```

the only way to break out of the loop is with a `break' statement.

The `continue' statement

The `continue' statement, when executed, starts executing the body of the loop over again from the top. For example, if we wanted to modify the last program to total only numbers greater than zero, we could write a program like this:

```c
#include <stdio.h>
int main(void)
{
        char line[100];  /* line for data input */
        int total;  /* running total of numbers */
        int item;  /* next item to add to list */
        int minus_items;  /* number of negative
    items */
        total = 0;
        minus_items = 0;
        while (1)
        {
            printf("Enter # to add\n");
            printf(" or 0 to stop: ");
            fgets(line, sizeof(line), stdin);
            sscanf(line, "%d", &item);
            if (item == 0)
                break;
            if (item < 0)
            {
                minus_items++;
                continue;
            }
            total += item;
            printf(Total: %d\n", total);
        }
        printf("Final total %d\n", total);
        return (0);
}
```

Chapter 15

ITERATIVE STATEMENTS IN C (PART II)

The while statement discussed in the previous chapter is an **entry-controlled loop** structure, in which the loop will not be executed if the test condition comes out to be false.

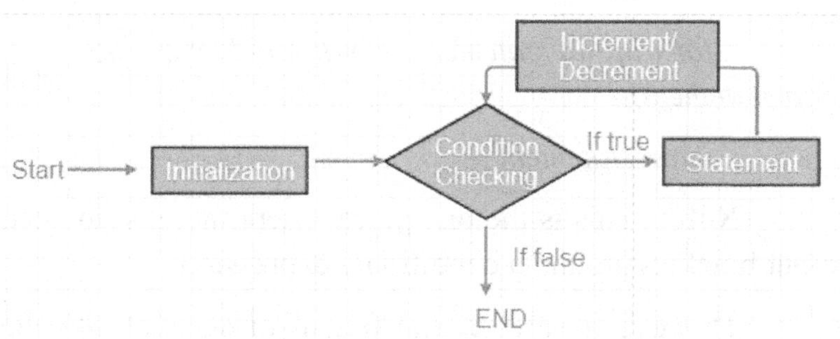

Flow Diagram of For Loop

In some cases, it might be necessary to execute the loop, even if the test-condition fails. So this kind of loops is called the **exit-controlled loop** structure. This takes the form:

> *do{*
>
>   *body of the loop*
>
>   *}*
>
> ***while*** *(test condition);*

Example:

> *do{*
>
>   *ch = getchar();*
>
>   *printf("The character entered is %c",ch);*
>
>   *}*
>
>   *while (ch != 'n')*

ch is assumed to be a variable of type character. Now the loop is executed first under no test and the input by the user is outputted. Then the entered value would be tested by the condition for further advancement.

The For Loop

The ***for*** loop is an entry-controlled loop that provides a more concise loop control structure. The general form of the ***for*** loop is:

> *for (initial statement; conditional expression; loop statement)*
>
> *main statement;*

Note: This is the one place where there is no need to put brackets around a conditional expression.

This executes the initial statement once, checks the condition and executes the main statement if the condition is evaluated to true, and then executes the loop statement. All three sections are optional so the following is allowed.

> *for (;;) mainstatement;*

It is an infinite loop as the conditional expression is always true if absent. This will keep executing main statement for ever.

The conditional expression is the most important of the three sections. As long as it is true the main statement is always run. Once the expression is false, the loop exits.

for (index=1 ;index <= 10;index++)

printf("The value of i is %i\n\r",i) ;

This outputs ten lines

The value of i is 1
The value of i is 2

..

The value of i is 10

index++ is shorthand for adding 1 to index. We could write **index = index + 1** or **index +=1** but **index++** is more concise.

Additional Features of for Loop

More than one variable can be initialized at a time in the *for* statement. For example:

for (p=1,n=0; n<18; ++n)

Like the initialization section, the increment section may also have more than one part. Here is an example:

for (a=2,b=30; n <= m; n=n+1,m=m-1){

p = b/a;

printf("%d ",p);

}

It is also permissible to use expressions in the assignment statements in initialization as well as in increment section. The following is a valid example:

for (w = (a+b); w>0; w=w/2)

One or more sections in the ***for*** statement can be omitted, if necessary. Here is an illustration:

e = 2;

for (; e != 10 ;){

    printf("%d",e);

    e = e + 2;

}

Both the initialization and increment sections are omitted in this ***for*** statement. In such cases, the sections are left blank. However, the semicolons separating the sections must remain. If the test-condition is omitted, the ***for*** loop will execute infinitely.

Chapter 16

DEFINING USER DEFINED FUNCTIONS IN C

A function is a sub program, which performs a specific task using the values given as input and then returns the result to the calling program.

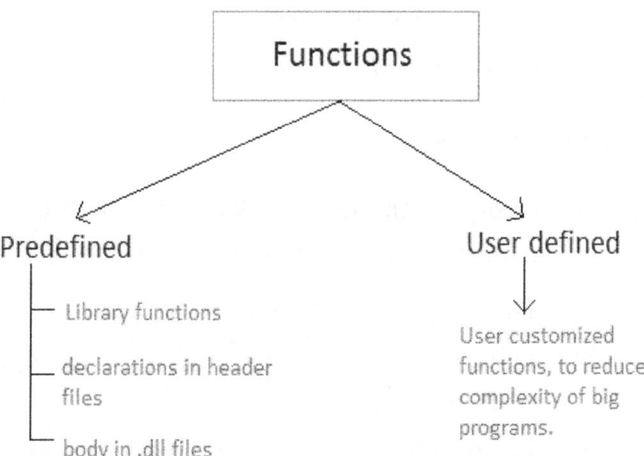

Types of Functions in C

Function contains a set of program statements that can be processed independently. When a function is invoked or called from other part of the program, it behaves as though its code is inserted at the point of the function call.

The program, which calls a function, is called as '*Caller*', and the function being called is known as '*Callee*'. The communication between the caller and the callee takes place through a set of variables called parameters. Functions are independent when the variables used within its body are local to it.

Every function has the following elements associated with it:

1. Function declaration or prototype

2. Function parameters (formal parameters)

3. Combination of function declaration and its definition

4. Return statement and

5. Function call

Function Prototype

This component is a declaration statement, which provides the following information to the compiler:

1. The name of the function

2. The type of the value returned (optional; default is an integer)

3. The number and types of the arguments that must be supplied in a call to the function

When a function call is encountered, the compiler checks the function call with its prototype in order to ensure that the arguments used in function call are of proper data type. The function prototype is having the following syntax:

ret_val   *function_name (argument 1, argument 2, ..., argument n);*

In this syntax, the ***ret_val*** specifies the data type of the value to be returned. When a function does not return any value, it must be specified with a keyword *void*. A void function can include a dummy *return* statement to return the control back to its caller without returning any value. The default return type is *integer*.

An example for function declaration is as follows:

int max(int x, int y);

In this example, *int* is the data type of the return value, *max* is the name of the function, and *x* and *y* are arguments of type *int*. It is also noted that the function declaration is end with a semicolon.

C makes prototyping mandatory if functions are defined after the function *main()*, i.e., after the function call. It assumes *void* in case of no arguments in the argument list.

Function Definition

The function itself is referred to as function definition. The first line of the function definition is known as function declarator or **function header** and is followed by the **function body**, which is enclosed in braces.

C allows the definition to be placed anywhere in the program. If the function is defined before its invocation, then its prototype declaration is optional.

Function body should contain a **return** statement to return the control back to its caller. The return statement can also be used to return the result of the function to its caller. When the return type is *void*, the function need not return any value, i.e., there is no need for a return statement within the function body. The following is the syntax for a function that doesn't return any value:

void fnName(param-list)

{

    statement(s)

    return;   *// return is optional*

}

Chapter 17

POINTERS AND ARRAYS IN C

A pointer is a variable used for storing the address of a memory location. Every pointer must be declared first before it is used in a program. This is due to the reason that a pointer can point only one type of data, just like a variable can hold only the data of a particular data type.

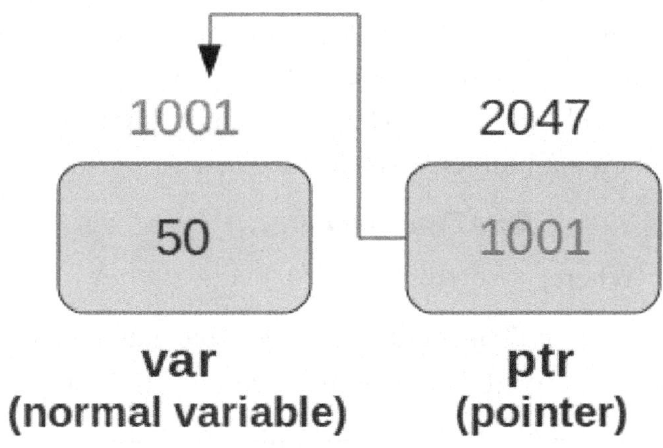

Use of Pointers in C

For instance, consider the pointer declaration given below:

int a;*

This statement declares *a* as an integer pointer that can hold only the address of an integer. Similarly a pointer to a float variable can point only a memory location that holds a floating point number.

The process of allocating memory space for variables during the course of program execution is called **dynamic memory allocation**. The other usages of pointers are as follows:

1. Accessing array elements

2. Passing arrays and strings to functions and

3. Creating data structures such as Linked List, Trees and Graphs.

Pointer Declaration and Initialization

Specifying the data type for the pointer is the first step involved in declaring a pointer variable. Before its declaration, we should determine the type of variable a pointer would point to. The following is the syntax given for declaring a pointer variable:

DataType* ptrVar, …;

Where,

i. *DataType* could be a primitive data type or user defined data type like Class or Structure

ii. *ptrVar* could be any valid C variable name.

In pointer declaration, the symbol * (called Asterisk) is used to inform the compiler that the variable declared (*ptrVar*) is a pointer variable. The pointer so created can hold the address of any variable of the specified type. Some typical pointer declarations are as follows:

int pmarks;*

char name;*

Date pDate;*

The first two declarations declare pointers of primitive data type, and hence the pointer *pmarks* can point only the variables of type *integer* and the variable *name* can point only a character. The third pointer variable is a pointer to a user-defined data type *Date*. Using it (*pDate*), we can point a date containing three fields: *dd, mm* and *yy*.

A pointer variable refers to a memory location, which contains the address of another memory location. Hence, after the declaration, a pointer must be assigned with an address of a memory location (or variable) so that it will point somewhere in memory. This can be done through code as follows:

*int marks, *pmarks;*

pmarks = &marks;

In the above example, *pmarks* is a pointer variable of type *integer* and *marks* is an ordinary variable that can store an integer.

After the declaration, the address of the variable *marks* is assigned to the pointer *pmarks* using the Address Opeartor (&) so that through pointer *pmarks* we can access the variable *marks*.

Dereferencing of Pointers

Dereferencing is the process of accessing and manipulating the data stored in the memory location pointed by a pointer. This process can be done through the use of Dereferencing operator * (asterisk). The operator * is used for both dereferencing as well as declaration of pointers. Example code for pointer dereferencing is as follows:

*int *pmark, mark;*

pmark = &mark;

**pmark = 100;*

*printf("%d", *pmark);*

In this example, the pointer *pmark* points to the integer variable *mark* that will hold an integer. Then the variable *mark* is assigned a value of 100 through the pointer variable *pmark* and a dereferencing operator. After the assignment of value 100, the same dereferencing mechanism is applied on pointer *pmark* to get the data of *mark* for output. Hence, the statement

*printf("%d", *pmark);*

has the same effect as in the following statement:

printf("%d", mark);

This task of accessing the data through pointers is also known as **indirect addressing**.

Arithmetic Operations on Pointers

While declaring a pointer variable, C insists that the pointer should be specified of a particular data type. For example, *int *pi;*

declares a pointer *pi* as not simply "a pointer", but "pointer to an integer". This is required for doing the arithmetic operations on pointers such as incrementing or decrementing the address of the pointer to refer to the next or previous locations of the current memory location indicated by the pointer.

If we consider that *pi* as a pointer to an integer, then *pi + 1* is the pointer to the integer immediately following the integer **pi* in memory, *pi - 1* is the pointer to the integer immediately preceding **pi*, *pi + 2* is the pointer to the second integer following **pi*, and so on.

Array and Its Operations

An array is defined abstractly as a finite ordered set of homogeneous elements. It is a data type, which is derived from primitive data types in C. The simplest form of an array is one-dimensional array. An example for one-dimensional array is a **String** of characters of size *n*, where *n* is the number of characters in the string.

The word '*finite*' in the above definition indicates that there is a specific number of elements in the array. The word '*ordered*' means the elements of the array are arranged so that there is a zeroth, first, second, third and so forth. By '*homogeneous*' we mean that all the elements in the array must be of the same type.

Array must be declared first, before we use it in a program. Declaring an array involves the following details:

    i.   Data type of the array

   ii.   Name of the array and

iii. Size of the array

Consider the following C statement, which declares an array of 100 integers:

int a[100];

There are two basic operations that can be done with an array: **Storing** and **Extraction** of items in the array. The storing operation is a function which accepts an array a, an index *i*, and an element x to store the value of x in *a[i]*. The storing operation is expressed as *a[i] = x*; whereas the extraction operation accepts an array a, and an index *i*, and returns an element of the array. It is expressed in C as *a[i]*.

Every array has got some limitation in storing its elements, i.e., it can store only a fixed number of elements. It's size or range is set by two limits called Upper Bound (UB) and Lower Bound (LB). The smallest element of an array's index is called its Lower Bound and in C is always 0, and the highest element is called its Upper Bound.

If L is the lower bound of an array and U is the upper bound, the number of elements in the array, called its range is given by (U-L+1). For instance, if L is 0, and the U is 99, then the range is 99-0+1 = 100. An important feature of a C array is that neither the upper bound nor the lower bound may be changed during the time of program execution.

Chapter 18

CHARACTER STRINGS IN C

A *Character String* is a sequence of characters that are stored in consecutive memory locations followed by a null character (\0). The null character has an ASCII code 0 and is called the end-of-string marker in C.

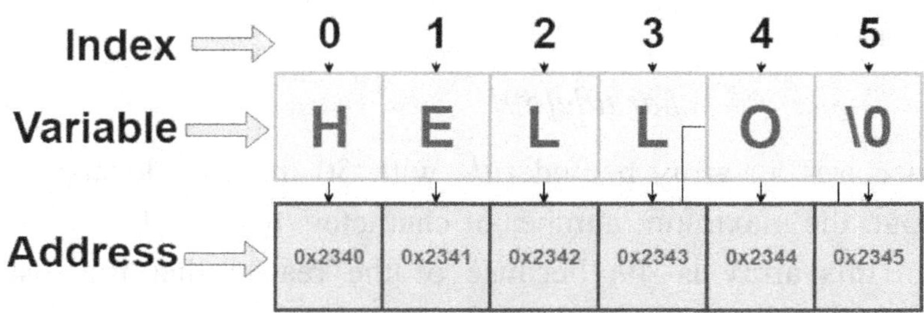

Handling Strings in C

Internally, each memory location of the above string "Hello" holds an ASCII equivalent of the respective character. The null character (a byte with value zero) is placed at the end of the string.

String constants are always enclosed in double quotes as follows:

"Hello, World!"

String constants are useful while conveying some message to the user. For e.g., the statement

Printf("Enter an ASCII code (0 – 127):");

will display the string (*Enter an ASCII code (0 – 127):*) on the screen. Strings are also used for storing and manipulating text such as words, names and sentences.

Declaring String Variables

A string variable is declared as one dimensional array of characters as follows:

char array-name[size];

where, *size* is an integer that specifies the length of the string. The maximum length of the string is always one less than the size (size-1), because one storage location must be reserved for storing the end of the string character. For instance,

char title[50];

declares an array named *title* with 50 memory locations. But, the maximum number of characters that can be stored in this array is 49, because of the reason that the last character should be an end-of-string character.

Another way of declaring a string is using **character pointer**. A pointer can be considered as an alternative to an array, because the name of the array itself is a pointer to the first location of the array. The following example illustrates this:

*char * title;*

title = "C Programming";

The above lines of code will declare a pointer variable of type *char* that points to the string "C Programming", which is stored in memory using consecutive memory locations. The pointer *title* points at the first character of the string, and it reads up to the end of the string for retrieving the string.

The input and output operations with strings through pointers can be done as follows:

*char * title;*

scanf("%s", title);

printf("%s", title);

Initializing Strings

Strings can be initialized at the time of its declaration using the following syntax:

char array-name[size] = {list of values separated by comma};

For instance, the statement:

char month[] = {'A', 'p', 'r', 'i', 'l', 0};

defines the string variable *month* and assigns to it the string "April.". The actual size of the string is 6. Because, the last character is 0 (zero), which indicates the end of the string and it occupies the last position of the character array. The end-of-string can also be marked with the character '\0'.

The end-of-string character must be given explicitly when the initialization is done character by character. But, for a string constant, it is assigned implicitly as in the following statement:

char month[] = "April";

In this case, the compiler takes care of storing the ASCII codes of the characters of the string in memory, and it assigns the NULL character at the end.

Chapter 19

DEFINING AND USING STRUCTURES

A structure is a group of items in which each item is identified by its own identifier called **member** of the structure. Each item in the structure may be of different types.

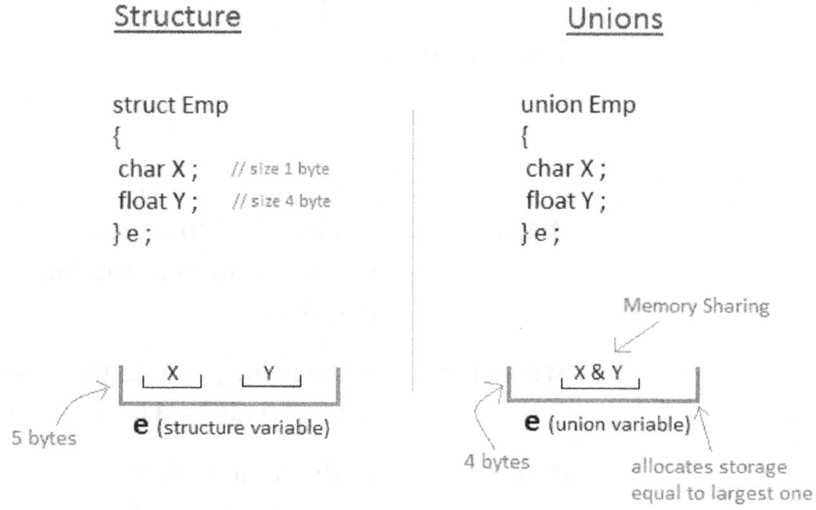

Difference between Structure and Union

Using structure data type, we can store a list of data items of a particular thing or person. Hence, in some programming languages, a structure is called as a '*Record*', and its members as '*Fields*'.

A Structure is also defined as a user-defined data type, which contains variables of different types in it. A group of variables are declared under the keyword **struct** and are called members of a structure. Each and every member is defined using a data type and a name. Following is the syntax for defining a structure and its members:

struct Struc_tag

{

datatype var-1;

datatype var-2;

...

...

datatype var-n;

}

} **Body** of the structure

where,

struct   -   is a keyword to indicate that the following is a structure definition.

Struc_tag -   is the name given to the new data type defined by the user.

Body   -   Body of the structure contains a block of declaration statements for defining a group of variables, which are enclosed within curly braces.

An example for a structure data type is as follows:

struct nametype

{

char first_name[10];

char midinit;

char last_name[20];

};

In this example, the name of the structure is *nametype*, which contains the members: *first_name*, *midinit* and *last_name*. The *first_name* and *last_name* are arrays of characters for storing the first and last name of a person, and the *midinit* is a character field for storing the initial.

Structure Variables

Structure variables are variables of type structure. Variables must be declared of a structure data type for making using of a structure and its members. A structure data type can't be directly used for storing values in its members; instead a variable of type structure can be used.

By declaring a structure variable, we allocate the memory locations for storing all the members of the structure in memory. The amount of memory required by a structure is the sum of the storage specified by each of its member types.

Structure variables can be declared in two different ways: Implicitly and Explicitly. In the first method, a variable can be declared in the structure definition itself.

At the end of the structure definition, i.e., after the closing brace of a new structure data type, we can include the structure variables for the same structure. The example for the first method is as follows:

struct nametype

{   char first_name[10];

char midinit;

char last_name[20];

} **name***;*

In the second method, we declare the structure variables in a separate line apart from the structure definition. First we define the structure, and then using that newly defined structure data type, we can declare structure variables any no. of times. Example for this method of defining structure variable is as follows:

struct nametype

{   char first_name[10];

char midinit;

char last_name[20];

};

struct nametype e_name, s_name;

In the above example, the structure type *nametype* is defined separately first. Then using it we have declared the structure variables e_name and s_name. The same structure *nametype* can also be used for declaring more variables later.

After declaring structure variables in a program, it can be used for storing values in it. Following is the notation used for accessing the members of a structure:

StrcutureVariable.MemberVariable;

Access the members of a structure using an operator called **dot** (.). Use the structure variable following by dot (.) and then the member variable for accessing or storing the values of a member. For the structure variables defined above, the members of which can be accessed like this:

e_name.first_name = "Rahul";

e_name.last_name = "Dravid";

s_name.first_name = "Sachin";

s_name.last_name = "Tendulkar";

*printf("%s %c %s", e_name.first_name, e_name.midinit,
e_name.last_name);*

ABOUT THE AUTHOR

J. David Livingston, a software professional turned academician, has been into teaching COMPUTER SCIENCE since 2003. He worked as an Assistant Professor in various Engineering Colleges affiliated to Anna University for 10 years.

He also worked as HOD in the Department of Computer Engineering in SRI Polytechnic College, Coimbatore. He has expertise in Programming Languages like C, C++ and Java, Client/Server programming, Web programming and Cloud Computing.

Book Written by the Same Author!

"ABCs of Cloud Computing" is a handbook written for the purpose of introducing the new technology called Cloud Computing to Students and Graduates who want to use it in their day-to-day life.

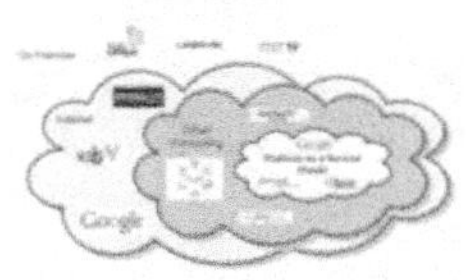

Welcome to FFY Center for Learning!

FFY CENTER for LEARNING is a platform where students are given training on the following:

- Structured Programming in C
- Object Oriented Programming in C++/JAVA
- Web Development using HTML/CSS/JavaScript
- Web Server Programming using PHP/MySQL
- Open Source Software Development using PHP/Perl/Python

Other Areas of Training:

- ✓ Communicative English
- ✓ Quantitative Aptitude

Made in the USA
Monee, IL
07 July 2026